The Grain Beneath the Gloss

poems by

Katherine Edgren

Finishing Line Press
Georgetown, Kentucky

The Grain Beneath the Gloss

Dedicated to my grandchildren:

Joshua David Lawson and Taya Danielle Lawson

ACKNOWLEDGMENTS

"Reverie on the Invisible Twitch" appeared in "Transports," a chapbook published
by Finishing Line Press in 2009, and also in "Water Music," The Great Lakes State
Poetry Anthology, published by the Poetry Society of Michigan, 2016.

"Tuesday Morning" appeared in "Bear Creek Haiku," October, 2005.

"After Vacation" appeared in "The Christian Science Monitor" August, 2005.

Publisher: Leah Maines

Editor: Christen Kincaid

Cover Art and Design: Cathy Doran-McMillion

Author Photo: Lucy Silverio

Printed in the USA on acid-free paper.
Order online: www.finishinglinepress.com
also available on amazon.com

Author inquiries and mail orders:
Finishing Line Press
P. O. Box 1626
Georgetown, Kentucky 40324
U. S. A.

Table of Contents

"There are mountains hidden in mountains,
there are mountains hidden in hiddenness."

Dögen

"How then, she had asked herself, did one know one thing or another
about people, sealed as they were?"

from *To the Lighthouse,* by Virginia Woolf

"the trick is to recognize a good thing when you saw it, no matter how
odd or worthless it might at first appear, no matter who else might just
walk away and leave it behind."

from *The Boys in the Boat,* by Daniel James Brown

Introduction

Jazz Singer

I'll carry my poise   with my music stand
    riff a wicked suite   front my own swing band.

        I'll wind and whirl through all that's jazz—
smooth-punk-cool-and-razzmatazz.

     My voiced verses'll   curve and flex
cartwheel   backbend   without license.

    I'll follow associations   on a whimsical vocation
  let hidden springs   fizz with sex.

I'll look for one thing   and find another.
    Strip   peel   and stumble upon
untangle the knotty   kiss the bonbon.

    In the kitchen-of-boogie   I'll lick off the sugar
shake-off the bitter   chew the hard-sticky   to the tender center.

I'll be the ground set free   of daffodil.
    Flamboyance-filled   my body language'll
       bray for me.

    I'll strip the moon of clouds
         enlarge the tiny
amplify the faint
     whip off the covers   raise the shades

   disclose wrinkled shivers in naked light
to find the pose within the poise.

      Fine-tuned to what's beyond
what's within   I'll open a drain   watch them slither and spin

  in the quest for a confessor to admire my sin.

1

Fascination

Prospecting

"I just couldn't stop gold from coming out of the ground."
Terry Herbert, discoverer of the Staffordshire Hoard in
2009, where he was searching an area of recently ploughed
farmland with a metal detector. Over the next five days,
enough gold objects were recovered from the soil to fill
244 bags.

I'm called by that magnetic vein that swims through ore,
    the glassy sap beneath the bark,
        the grain beneath the gloss.

Buried treasure's charm is like the burr that grips
    or the knot that begs untangling.

I hunt clods for crystals, hammer geodes, splash
    bland stones exposing the gild of old honeycombs.

I split the milkweed's clever seam, and find it stuffed with surprise—
    silky white feather-fluff poised for springing.

I part winter's branches—safes for cunning nests—
    to release gold dust that's been concealed.

I'm lured like a famished fish.
    I seek the strange within the same.

Wandering the forest path, I spy a cottage window—
    yellow lit, a kernel within a shell—
        and break trail to get to the glittering nut.

I tamp down what allures, bury my head, tell myself
    it's unworthy, obvious, unsophisticated—

        yet I'm tumbleweed in a desert wind.
I won't be satisfied until—
    will always cock an ear, unless—

Like gold, like an insistent wink, the gleam persists.
Even in sleep, the beckoning invades,

and I rush toward this drug:

deliver me of this gold.

Scraping

*a haibun**

Grasping the metal scraper with both hands, I scrub the siding. It's hard, muscular work felt in the triceps. I claw at the wall to get into the paint with this tool that extends my reach, and gives me greater power. Scraping is linear: I take one board and follow it to the wall's end, work the scraper into crevasses and slanted places on the board's edge. The rhythm travels up arms into chest—the way parade drums invade a body—as legs hold me firm. When I reach a spot where paint is wearing off, the scraping is like scratching an itch.

The Forest Service dictates cabin colors, with greens and browns the only choices. Doc and Ethel chose green, and they painted the first, buoyant coat in the early 50's, when I was in elementary school, and my husband-to-be was a young teen. After marrying into the family, I've painted more than once. Today, I scrape to create a surface ready for priming, necessary for protection and absorption. In some places, I find the wood goes punk with age, softening and dampening toward rot. Found there under all those layers. Subterranean. Some wood is still fine, unvanquished by Minnesota weathers. I am only a few years older than this cabin.

I look for the plain board, the pine wood, the local trees that made this cabin, the wood grain underneath. I destroy to rebuild, uncover to re-cover, as

> paint falls
> in green shades
> the smallest flecks carried off by light winds
> to join pollen
> dragonflies
> smoke   ashes.

A Japanese form that combines prose and one or more haiku, with variations in form.

The Humongous Fungus

We know from scientists that the *Armillaria Bulbosa*
lives under a forest near the Wisconsin border.
Thirty-eight acres big and still growing,
it weighs as much as an adult blue whale,
and is over 1500 years old.
Residents of Crystal Falls, Michigan celebrate it in August
at the Humongous Fungus Festival,
where local merchants cash in with Fungus Burgers,
Fungus Fudge, and T-shirts.
Everyone shares a Humongous Mushroom Pizza.

Neither Yeti nor Nessie, but still a hidden giant
the underground parts are unseen. Yet we believe in them.
Not that it's too small to see. It's too buried,
so we take it on faith, except in the fall, when the fungus' tiny
edible honey mushrooms poke through the ground
like slender fingers—and wave hello—as evidence.
          Would they taste like chicken?

Though growing underground, it's not a bulb,
and makes no flowers.
There's no seismic shift. Instead
it's diaphanous, mycelial,
a biological buried treasure,
a white fire kindling imagination.
Like snake or mole, or ants building cities,
it pushes past roots and glacial erratics
to find and claim its place.

The subterranean fungal web limns
all buried worlds, deeds undone,
words unsaid, everything and everyone
forgiven and unforgotten, all there is that can't
be seen or felt, every contradiction
every conviction,
the earth beneath me spinning.

Magician

Old Towne's crowded on New Year's Day.
A man with a beard sits at the bar beside an empty stool.
Empty, except for a red scarf that holds the seat
as taken, so I slide into the only one left.
John stands by me. We order two pints,
and sip drafts to country songs of heartbreaking love.
From time to time, I turn to look, but
no one takes the empty stool.

Is this the scarf his lover dropped like a hankie—
all that's tangible of her memory?
Or does he wait for someone he knows
or might meet? A blind date?
(*I'll be at the bar beside a red scarf*).
Maybe someone slipped out the back door
and left the scarf in her disappointed wake.

Could it be a ruse to keep others away?
Perhaps he doesn't like the look of us, claims
breathing room, as he spreads out
and asserts himself in the New Year.

No. He's a desperate magician
who's pawned his whole kit.
The scarf is all that's left from his hat:
wand, coins, ropes, cards, the whole abracadabra.

It's an empty fishing line, a stand-in
for all the ones he couldn't reel in
kept for comfort and company
as he empties glass after blurring glass.

At the break, he's gone.
His stool and the one next to it
now filled by a smiling couple.

Ah, first, sweet mystery of the year
hummed in silent harmony
with all that's lost and pawned.

Reverie on the Invisible Twitch

Dedicated to Bruce Wolfgram

My fingers circle the rod in supplication
      for the quick jink of fish bite—

like hands on the Ouija board's pointer, as a child—
      I still wait for the twitch of the invisible.

But now

it's fish, not predictions, that I divine,
      as we troll gently, motor murmuring.

*

Sometimes my bait drags on bottom so weedy
      it mocks the perch bite
and tricks me into setting the hook.

A kind of electricity
      echoes up the line, tingles through the rod
and into my hands.

My dulled head blazes
      with the mystery underneath the calm.

And when a fish finally does bite,
      it is like the feet of a fetus, flutterkicking.

If the male of our species wants to know that illegible tug,
      he needs only to fish.

*

Some are timid lickers or samplers,
                others, bold yankers and runners.

Some travel companionably in schools,
                                        others are loners.

Some are ancient,
                        others, too small to keep.

                                *

The great Mississippi channels through the lake like a road
                carrying bizarre, giant fish on long journeys, stoking dreams.

Perhaps there will be a fish so big it will break my line, or pull my rod
                        into the water: a Muskie—fish of a thousand casts!

                                *

The lake is fed by fishermen
and decorated with lost lures and lines,
the smoothed branches of old trees.
We coast in the middle—sky above—water below—
three connected universes teeming with creatures.

                                *

We wait for hours—doing without doing.
                Looking down, it grows too dark to see.

Flicking on running lights, we find ourselves
                just one in a twinkling community on this dark land of water,

lungs open,
                practicing optimism, learning hope.

Glimpses

Petoskey Stones

Before it was a mitten, Michigan was anchored
in a warm shallow sea below the equator
where coral fed on plankton,
their bodies huddled in colonies.

When the sea withdrew, minerals swept in
and transformed the coral communities
into fossils made of calcite, quartz, pyrite.

Slowly, tectonic plates made their move.

Then, glaciers strode over everything,
plucking up hard fossils from bedrock, breaking, flinging,
scattering them like seeds all over Michigan.

Oceans and ice masses, weather and sand
smoothed and rounded their jagged edges,
and when the people finally came,

they called them *Petoskey,*
after the settlement on the big lake named in of honor the father who—
seeing his child for the first time, rays of sun in his face—
called him *Petosegay:* Rising Sun.

Discovered best in early spring after ice
pushes a new crop to shore. Found too,
in ditches, road beds, gravel pits, and rock shops.

Dull-gray and unremarkable when dry,
wet, these coral tombs bloom
into startling honeycombs of stone.

Bent backs aching, eyes smarting, patient ones
find and collect these coral-fossils,
and polish or show them in water-filled bottles
to call attention to their detail.

Each white hexagon contains a dark spot—
once a mouth—now filled with stone.
Despite their silence, these ancient mouths speak to me
of a raw, untarnished world.

Facts

Early scientists thought a sperm
was a homunculus:
a fully-formed, tiny human being
hiding in the testes.

First Look at Cass Lake

unfocus and see

crushed foil,
the silvery landscape

the elephant,
and all the muscles
undulating beneath the skin

Wind Chill: 15 Below

Steam shadows strobe and billow, flash
on the snow-field in the hard noon light.
Blown-gauze suggests a hazy nuance of mist.
All hoods are up, fashion sacrificed to comfort,
with only small ovals exposed, each pinched face
surrounded by a puckered parka.

Back home, a tufted titmouse faces the light.
He blends in with the gray, puffs up like a tennis ball,
with shoulders hunched to cheeks.
Evergreens are blue against the white.
Hidden deep in their dark branches
are all the twitchy sparrows,
suave juncos, and plump doves
now anchored and concealed from the wind
like me.

March Fields

Field after field resembling the backs of animals—
cats or dogs, deer or moose, coyote or wolf

with their curves and furs,
browns and beiges, drabs and duns
leaping beside the car.

I ache to stroke them
the way I'd stroke a tame beast
making that smooth, dipping motion,
perhaps scratching under a chin.

Some so soft.
Rough ones prickle a palm.

My hands must grow enormous,
or the fields must shrink.

Lacking this magic,
suffused with March fields,
my eyes do the stroking.

Lost and Found

"86% of land species and 91% of marine species
are still out there waiting for names"
        from a 2011 study by Camillo Mora,
        New York Times: 5-27-14

The 40 foot tall Dragon Tree* was known to natives of Thailand,
but was neither named nor classified until 2014.
That same year, concealed in transparency,
new-fangled shrimp were found swimming near Santa Catalina Island.

Some species may be hidden because of their smallness,
or because they were never imagined,
like the *Tinkerbella nana*—the Costa Rican fairy fly—
as long as one-third the thickness of a credit card—
or the slight, blind snail with the pale shell
found dallying in a Croatian cave.

As species disappear, there is consolation
in undiscovered insects, arachnids, bacteria and viruses,
plants and animals, as yet unnamed.

We live in the beat before the knowing and the naming.

        * *The Dracaena kaweesakil*

Atonement and Ambivalence

Myths

My house contains a bookshelf
with an inner and an outer row.

In front on public view are myths I've constructed:
that I'm kind and good, organized and industrious;
a good Mom, wife, daughter, sister, friend.

In back are books of hard truths I'd rather forget.

I take down these hidden books, open their creaky bindings,
and remember the words of a former boss:

You must have done something very bad to have to atone so much.

The Swan

Milky veined quartz
glides on winter's back.

Tucked wings—
frozen carnations,
iceberg fragments,
jagged glass.

Beware
the swan that lures you,
that blurs your eyes with beauty,
then bites you.

Apologies

for scaring a little girl with my big girl voice

for frightening my daughter right into her closet with her blanket

for ripping off the band-aid of lies: telling my son
about the Easter Bunny, Santa, and the Tooth Fairy
all at once

for storming into the room of two giggling girls
who wouldn't let me sleep

for cruelty to friends

for pointing out *the woman with the eyebrows.*

Sometimes I'm unable to suppress the wild bull
that stomps its feet amidst the wreck.

Deep

I have no idea how deep it is.
        I see only the top
and have to guess, plumb, or jump in
        and note the time it takes to touch.

I assume it's not bottomless;
        I can handle what's over my head.
I wonder if I have enough breath
        to descend, and come back up again.

I'm a Flea

*With gratitude to Akiko Busch for the inspiration from
"How to Be Invisible," New York Times, 2-8-2015*

No one sees me.
I inhabit anonymity.
Tucked into its pocket
I fit perfectly.

Atop my steed and full of glee
I'm an inconspicuous marvel,
a hard-bodied defier of notice.

Though I see you, you can't see
my elegant legginess, so useful
for agility; my piercing mouth-parts
that possess a delicate beauty.

Small in a big world,
my size grants special sight.
I ride dog with calm aplomb
gaze down from great height.

Asserting existence wouldn't be wise
and like the Zen Master—
or a gray mouse in a feedbag—
I stand out of the way, in disguise.

Hanging on, burrowed in
I endure, bend a knee,
gratefully lisping a prayer for my place
in the scheme of dog and flea.

When dog moves, I cast no shadow—
a high-jumper in the luxury of dog-fur meadow,
imprint of extravagant obscurity—
that's me.

Dog senses merely
the suggestion of me
waffling through thick fur
like a summer breeze.

Profoundly poised,
light and composed,
I'm confident in camouflage, liberated, freed
by the grace and glory of going unseen.

Concealment

Mushroom

Elegant, empty table in the woods. Palest yellow.
With a flutelike stem, the neck of a snowy egret.
Audrey Hepburn balancing a wide hat on a small
head. Sudden beauty for a day or two. With an intact
          subterranean life
          unseen. Pretending
          nothing's tangled
          beneath. Hiding
          an underside
          of folds and gills.
          Asserting itself.
          As if mother said:
          chest out, chin up.
          As if it lacks
          the fragility
          of an unbaked
          pie crust, or a small
          raw mammal
          from an eagle's view.
          So easily toppled
          and torn, so easily
          ripped by wind
          or the foot of
          a running chipmunk.
          Lifted, like a ballerina,
          Lifted into sky, like
          the arms of trees.
          Lifted up,
          a brave offering.

The Gift of Warning

It came to me last night in a dream,
how grateful I am for the gift of warning—
the time stubbed toe's pain needs
to travel to the brain, or the growling
within the thundercloud—so we brace before the rain.

Instead of the instant ugly blow, trip wire, stumble-fall, slip,
warning buttresses the shock or faint,
stiffens spine and upper lip,
so I run into a softer wall.

I prefer the gradual weakening of my mother's still-heard voice,
the rising rejection of food, the lack of desire for news,
the sizzling out of synaptic fire
in days of aimless dawdle,

this creeping murmur, this slow unravel—
like the pucker of white on the river's skin that outs the submerged rock—
or the reflective pause providing occasion
for saying what can be said with modulation, moderation.

I prefer the unhurried charge of time's collapse,
confusion's deepening, as she makes her way
into the dark skirmish, cresting still breathless plateaus,
oases of thinking, islands of light.

Cracks widen, fissures lengthen in the slow slouch of reveal
where, too dark to play
all that was hidden and sought finally flies home
Olly Olly Oxen free!

Blue

Blue flash slices air, lights
the hedgerow in my path.

Deep blue
bird of the iridescent song

clear-cut as cloud edges
seen from an airplane.

Known again:
the indigo bunting

my Dad's favorite bird.
His sharp blue eyes

would spy it, his
voice catching at his luck.

And Christmas lights, too.
He, who did not often insist,

insisted on dressing each tree
in blue lights only, something understood

by his children, later huddled outside
in dark cold, to gather the effect.

Here today,
transformed into this small blue

bird he joins me on my path
with his luminous liquid code

catching me in his blue net,
his song so focused, so purely itself.

Burying

My dog knows the pleasures of shoving nostrils into dirt
savory with hint of squirrel or woodchuck,
grabbing and flinging cool ground with her paws,
dropping the clenched bone,
and using her head as a shovel to disguise the hole.

Not to mention the fun of digging it up again.

She loves the whole game: burying for later,
hiding her prize from someone else,
and sometimes even hiding it from her forgetful self.

Watching, I wonder: how to disentangle instinct from desire?

Does the dog desire to bury its bone?
Does the ant desire to carry its load?
Or are they compelled by something merely programmed
through millennia of evolution?
Unknown, but intimate, tied into its smallest parts.

Does instinct merge with desire?

Do I merely label a lower animal's desire *instinct*,
as I call my own, higher instinct *desire?*

I bury too, and sometimes forget what and where,
but bury to avoid pain,
more than for the joy of it.

It seems instinctual to bury what would disturb,
paralyze or immobilize.

Anger, grief, and horror can be tamped down
so deeply I never confront them.

I bury them for the worms to devour,
leaving nothing
but dirt.

The Ballad of Sandra Bland

Heading to a job at Prairie View
she landed in the County Jail.
If she'd been white, she'd be alive,
instead of under the coffin nail.

A feisty, young black activist—
a firebrand, you understand—
if it's meekness that you seek
turn away from Sandra Bland.

College degree-summer counselor-
volunteer-in a band-
a brilliant job starting soon:
the criminal past of Sandra Bland.

Driving through Waller County
she met her nemesis.
Just once she didn't signal,
this: the awful genesis.

On her way and full of life
failure to show a change in lane
warped into a capital offense
after a heated exchange

with Brian Encinia, Texas Cop,
whose version of respect—
what he said that he most wanted—
extinguishing her cigarette.

Exit the car he ordered,
taser in his hand.
His eyes grew wide: *I'll light you up!*
Who's your Master, Sandra Bland?

A taser delivers compliance
using fiery electroshock

subduing what's highly dangerous:
unneeded in a traffic stop.

He tossed her to the dirty ground,
the way to command respect.
He turned into a two-bit tyrant,
his knee upon her neck.

She was a wily fish
wriggling on the handcuff-hook.
In netting this scrappy specimen,
he threw away the book.

And he arrested her.
Pulled over for a traffic violation.
On her way, full of life—
soon: a wrongful death investigation.

They took her to a Texas jail.
Twenty-eight, and far from home.
Why oh why she asked again?
They tossed her in a cell, alone.

*How did failure to signal
turn into all of this?*
We failed you, Sandra Bland
in this nightmare of madness.

At 9 am the jailer found her
hanging in her cell,
hanging from a garbage bag.
She'd known some kind of hell.

Those who knew her cried *foul play.*
The jailors named it suicide.
In one upbeat about her job,
her friends suspected homicide.

A soldier and an warrior in the
BLM campaign; never lazy.
Depression, THC in her blood—
they tried to call her crazy.

Dash cam tapes showed up: edited.
The truth remains a mystery.
The jail failed a suicide watch.
We hold her now in memory.

The family was paid a settlement.
Injustice *had* stalked the land.
The cop was fired, taser retired.
Black Lives Matter, Sandra Bland.

Now all across this murderous land,
as people roam the street,
we sing an elegy for Sandra Bland.
Without justice, there is no peace.

Descent

Mother's Day

Dinner out with family, wine and key lime pie,
armloads of colors and cards and hugs.
Still,

eyes too wide, mouth tense,
(most evident in photographs).
Her grinning bares too many teeth, as if in defense.

Her mind has grown crazed like old bone china
that could easily slip into, then off of a lap.
Poised for shattering.

Now, her words of wanting to *leave before too long*—
take me back to when I was thirteen
when she often spoke of suicide

and how, not to worry,
she wouldn't get blood on the carpet.

Back then, she made lists as she planned her funeral:
no Cadillac would bear her body,
a rosebush by her grave, requiring perpetual care.

I was afraid
to come home from school.

Fear once instilled
takes a long time to leave

like the hatched bug in Thoreau's table
gnawing its way out.

Wounded

Though the trajectory's path leans toward healing,
the body holds what it sustains—
whiplash suffered in a childhood wreck
translates decades later to a stiff neck

knockings and gougings from hurdle-running
demand new knees in your seventies—
dancing on pointe while young trips up when bones crack,
and the big toe grows in-elastic

the skiing incident on the hill:
source of the retina's slow peel?
seeds planted in sun—regretted sin—
yield wrinkles, cataracts, cancerous skin

hurt feelings too deep for healing's tender reach
tend to swell-pinch, punch-itch
with no chance to relax or scratch;
while fear, shame, anger, and grief merely nap

before they snap erect.
No dam can halt this downstream flow,
its current too swift for any filtering gauze.
Which lasting wound was made by which gash

can be untraceable, track-less.
Still, each lesion leaves a permanent stain,
like a whisper in the genes, or like original sin,
first carved in bone, then sealed in.

I cradle my injuries so long they grow heavy.
Skin thins, an opening forms;
injuries force their way out of this chink
to ripen, rot, stink.

I am softening inside, like clay,
molded, dented
by clumsy thumbs.

How to Form a Perfect Callus

If you play the cello, you need a callus.
Sharp strings cut plushy fingertips.
Dilettantes and dabblers grow discouraged.

Build a hard callus, take the long view,
or you'll find an oozing blister instead.

A tough callus deadens feeling,
the way a mute dampens the trumpet's stab.

As the coming cold nudges the dog to add a fine fur,
night dreads, too, call for the cultivation of a second skin:

the callus of letting go, the callus of not my problem,
the callus of I can't do anything about it.

I've built so many—on fingertips, heels,
and in my mind—barricading places I won't go.
Callus-like blinders can obscure horrors,
if I'm careful where I look.

When I was a child, my mother's pain pressed
into my skin like a cello string, forming a callus:
my vow never to be like her.

The Subterranean Splinter Blues

I.
Living under my skin for days, resembling a smaller version
of the cyst I'd worn on my back like a homunculus, alien invader.
Like a tooth with a dying root, or a low-grade infection,
the splinter hides until the body confesses it.

Splinters make me wonder about all the other festerings
under the prison of my skin   my mind.
Unknowns I choose not to explore.
Everything erased from conscious memory, everything ignored.

The day's images picked up like sticktights
                              rise up in the night, and turn
into flooding water
                    a car with no brakes
          a chase
                    the stranger's face.

II.
Sometimes too small to bother until it insists—
like the bass rapping in the stop-light car, a hungry baby.

A fragment germinates and blooms into petals of pain.
          The lion is brought low by the thorn.

How can something so small be so loud?

III.
Mere chip, flake, scrap, bit,
a needling sliver of silver makes a point.

A shiver of a sliver nags:
that call I haven't made,
          that note I didn't send,
                    that unexpressed complaint.

Bias too. And regret.

Painful. Hard to remove.

Latching tick, burrowing worm, looping tape.

There's no mute button for this nagging.
          No earplugs, no numbing drug.

IV.
Wood from railing or picnic table,
or glass from something shattered and forgotten
would dig into toughest skin
and be loyal—until expelled, divorced.

It didn't belong and couldn't flourish:
irreconcilable differences.

V.
Slivers from barefoot-walking need soaking,
a sterilized needle, tweezers with a steady hand.
Nurse-Mother digs deeper with a needle,
and I, the splinter-bearer, hold my breath,
steel for necessary pain.

But ah, the flood of relief!
Suffused with brandy-heat,
redemption with removal.

VI.
Sometimes it cooperates and works its way out.
          Sometimes it comes out in pieces.
                    Sometimes it leaves a mark beside a memory.

VII.
Off in the distance, I watched valleys splintering with spires.
          Was I once part of a whole that splintered off?

Ashes

first, a brother
then, a mother

over the lee side, disappearing under the boat, and we could see them
on the other side, drifting

billowing, billowing, falling over and under themselves
like gray clouds, or smoke, or sound rolling, swelling
under the surface of the lake,
eliminating all history of the body

there was comfort in the billowing,
and the way the lake took the ashes so quickly,
dispersing, incorporating,
folding them in

Modulations

Going to Church

When I was young, we wore girdles to church
whether we needed them or not.
This was before the garter belt. Before panty hose.
Nylons replaced anklets at 6th grade graduation—
a hard-fought battle to sacrifice comfort for seeming grown up.

Even on boiling hot Sundays we'd all perform the same pre-church ritual,
dragging our girdles up over our feet, like pale dead alligators,
where they'd snap, as if they still had some life in them.
They squeezed our bottoms into the same unnatural shape—
one giant, heart-shaped teardrop,
flattening our womanly organs,
making it hard to take a deep breath.
Any faint stirrings were effectively quashed
under itchy steel bands encircling the nether regions.

Ostensibly for holding up our nylons,
girdles were white armor
holding sex at bay
in a hot church.

How early we learned our moral duty
to protect men from themselves,
to refrain from putting temptation in their way.

Frailty

The pew is made hard to remind us to listen.
Peppermint wafts through the air.

I sit behind my Sunday school teacher
and sometime church organist
whose beige dress complements her blonde hair in sunlight
streaming through stained glass windows.
Close enough to touch,
her slender, zippered back is posture perfect.
Her name is Faith.

From the pulpit, black and purple robes flowing,
forehead glistening, black hair and eyebrows,
heavy stubble despite the morning shave,
he's been up for hours, finishing his sermon.
He seems to be talking to me.
His voice penetrates, brings me God's anger.
Faith trembles.
His name is John.

One morning over scrambled eggs, my parents reveal
that Faith and John have run away together
forsaking the church, her husband, two teenagers, his wife,
all his children,
and taking her last child; their love-child.
My fork clangs as I lose my appetite
along with my faith.

Rumor had it, they'd being doing it on the catechism class table.
(It had been going on for years.)

A sinner, forced to leave the church,
fated to drive a Yellow Cab.
The homeless at a mission became his flock.
There, he served up blessings with the soup
before resuming an eternal search for fares.
What became of her, we never knew.

Christmas Eve Choir

The tenors wore tuxedos. Except for the one
who wore a suit—the countertenor.
They'd been saving them, concealed in plastic
beside their wives' wedding dresses.

We closet dress-up clothes for the special moments
which otherwise pass us by, unmarked.
Honors, weddings, the choir at Christmas.

May our lives be filled with occasions graced with tuxedos.

Occupations

I'm a jeweler magnifying miniature faces with my monocular loupe.
I'm an archeologist deciphering facts from artifacts.
I'm a graphologist inspecting sense within the script,

an anthropologist among aborigines, connecting meaning with found bones,
a surgeon carving away in exploratory surgery,
a de-coder, turning what's messy into messages.

Secret Stuff

I. Kinds

Escalating deafness.
The urge to suffocate a sleeping spouse,
to turn away from a Messianic boss.
Jealousy felt toward a lucky friend.
Coveting the neighbor's job, that house.

Even the way he mumbles to himself
when he thinks he's alone.
Or how she wants to cuddle with her blankie at her age.
He can't find his way home.

Telling her of the affair would lift the weight of guilt,
but would hurt her, if he spoke.

Then there are the worst things I've ever done,
broken promises,
the times I failed in being kind:

secrets without reason
that would wilt and wither me
in their light.

II. Pleasures

Gifts unwrapped when all alone
considered in bliss or scandalous secret,
the pleasures of the body.

Going without underwear
or singing a public solo—
            better than I could ever imagine.

Not having to tell my story
to someone who's been there.

Successfully biting my tongue
with the parents of my grandchildren.

These secrets are comforting treasures
that distinguish me.

Journeys

(It hides in a new poetic form) The Golden Shovel Form Poem*

With Gratitude to John Keats ("To Autumn")

There's a place rampant with fruitfulness,
sharp rays of sun
poking through rooms and yard, rays that bless
me as I run
round apple trees
to find the fattest fruit and toss the core
to ground to lie among the walnut shells—
some squirrel-cracked—but always, there are more.
I'll lounge on the deck among the furry bees
inhabiting the picnic-table frame; they never cease.
Their buzzing infiltrates my summer cells.

Aromas of fruit and sun, apples and bees I'll store
away for winter's mind where I shall find
them beside the fire, as I lie upon the floor
listening to the wind
as I gradually slip asleep,
pulled off the waking stage by a hook
once used for weeding beds of flowers.
I'll drowse and keep
these memories, and read beside a dreamy brook,
a book upon which grateful eyes will look,
and keep grand company for hours.

And where are they who feel the same way too?
Who save up the graces of the day,
blessings of the finest hue?
Who also mourn
the seeds that fly aloft,
the rose that dies,
while cares are bourn
by fleeing birds, their rowing wings soft
over field and croft
ere vanishing in graying skies?

* A form developed by Terrence Hayes, where you choose a poem and use the last word of each line of the poem for the last word of each line of your poem, which can be about something totally different from the original poem. You credit the poet.

Body Language

The Eskimos—now properly called Inuit—
had a custom of sharing their spouses with a guest.
The female guest would nestle snug and nude
between two caribou skins, and if the husband approached
she was to raise her eyebrows if interested,
and if not, frown, and purse her lips.

My informant, an elderly lady with white hair
reported this anthropological tidbit to us
over trifle at a banquet,
having spent four years in the Arctic
as a school teacher.

She said that one day
an Inuit man took her in his arms
and refused to loosen his grip.
She frowned but he wouldn't, or couldn't see,
and so she screamed *No! No!*
until he understood.

When she reported this event to the priest
he inquired whether she
had shared any meals with the man.
She had.

You must have given him a message
with your cutlery, he said.
Perhaps the circling motion you made
as you stirred sugar into tea?
Or the extra flourish made with your wrists?
The way you held the knife
scrubbing it back and forth
to cut the tough meat?

After her story, we wondered
how a priest came across these bits,
but will surely monitor our use of cutlery
if ever we visit the Arctic.

An Assay: On Finding

Hungry to see the elusive moose,
I feed my appetite with other sights.

Some treasures are there for the noticer;
others require a search party.

I might need a shovel to find the gold.

Some scatter hints, like bread crumbs.
Some require faith in their existence.

Some are so well-hidden, I don't know to look,
and miss the epiphany's gleam, as it glides off stage.

Some I simply overlook, like the *sparassis radicata,*
the edible cauliflower mushroom, or any food
safe for foraging. Earthy flavors,
extravagant and wild, sadly go to waste.

I have to learn what to look for before I can fully see.

Sometimes I neglect one thing as I focus on another:
the eagle above the lake,
while I admired the iris on shore.

My focus and attention are limited.
I can't see both macro and micro.

Some things hide so well, I can only wonder if they exist
(the yeti, the Loch Ness Monster, inter-stellar life.
True love, redemption).

Some bury themselves a long, long time and emerge years later:
like shingles,
anger, jealousy, or regret.

Sometimes ears and nostrils, taste buds and pores

shut against the nudge, the bird's clear note.

Blinders are too tight so I only look ahead,
and miss the sunset behind. I can't see
what runs beside me.

Sometimes I find what I'm
not looking for.
Sometimes it finds me.

After Vacation

Reeds inhabit, then hold
the direction of the wind
as they bend toward shore.

The tiller,
the fishing pole, the handlebars
still inhabit my curled fingers.

Revelations

This Morning, My Father

The wind is my Father pushing the snow,
the way he swept bangs off my forehead to wake me—
covering and uncovering, shaping and re-shaping
the drowsy world hidden under sleep.

I listen to my Father's words:
whether flung into vast escaping sky,
or slipped into the envelope sealed by the sea's blue flap,
know I accompany you in your fragile song.

I remember the turnings of days on earth,
how the lindens were laced with snow,
the way trillium lit the forest path.

I won't forget the scrap of blue with wings,
and that my death was a thief of quiet.
Now, I know a small part of the invisible.

I'd waltz with you to the tune of it, if I could.
I'd brush your bangs off your forehead again to wake you,
to share secrets with you dear one, if I could.

Early Frost

Promised frost pries us from recliners,
sends jazz and jimmy into limbs,
springs us out-of-doors to rescue
plants we love or tolerate
too frail for crystal layers. We lift, lug,
and line them up in the sun-warmed garage:
our poor man's conservatory.

Inspecting this plant limbo, we marvel
at the spongy, red-tinged lobes of the jades—
a sea of ears straining to hear summer's sun.
Examining leafy undersides
of the triple-blooming hibiscus, we search
for miniscule, white, resolute bugs.

And then, we notice the sea onion's long, inexplicable, reaching branch,
    end-tipped
with a spray of white.
Travelling down
the green limb's length, we
are nudged backwards
in a time machine.
First, fresh flowers,
then dried.
Further down
flowers transformed
into fists of
green seedpods,
next to
pods turning brown.
Closest to the mother plant
open pods, sere,
seeds dispersed.

A gawping archeology,
a window into the past,
a life-line where time's

layered trail is found
in quadruple exposure,
a panorama made manifest
on a green, ungainly bough
that we never would've noticed
if not for the revelations
of frost.

October Morning Turnings

Frost-salt jewels milkweed pods.
Overhead, wild cries of geese resemble sirens.
Autumn's trees are immolations of a sort.
Sweet rot of fallen apples blends with skunk's defense.
White-rimed arms of leaves splay stiff upon the ground.
Asparagus fronds catch light and toss it back, glistening.
My pup noses ghost-footprints from the night before.
A pair of Sandhills frost-gray
are camouflaged on a neighbor's lawn—
but for masked faces anointed with daubs of red.
Their angled knee-hinges swivel
as they balance on one leg, tuck the other inside warm feathers,
then switch legs.
After straining at the leash,
my nonplussed pup composes herself to watch.
Their trills ricochet off houses surrounding the pond.
Keening for their tribe?
Echoes make them sound more than two.
Grass blades bristle in evergreen shade until
that rayed yellow eraser turns grizzled lawns
to wet prisms.

Margaret's Garden

Beneath the snow, the hellebore
is a kept secret:
a paramour
waiting for the perfect moment
to disclose her splendor.

Lake in Star Island

I wade in the cool pool of mysteries
that tickle my ankles, nip at my feet.

I bend over and try to catch
what lives beneath with my sieve-hands

but they slip through,
vanish into silty bottom.

I sink to my calves.

The silky water runs through me.

First Snow

My dog barrels toward me—
a fullback running for a touchdown.
Clutched in her teeth, the neon green Frisbee—
like a bright wing of a caught parrot—
so big, she can hardly manage. She has it
by the edge—a stiff flag
nearly covering her face; next she's
a tribal Ethiopian with a full lip plate—now
the curtain of snow so thick
I can barely see her
and it's just us in the driving snow
tails wagging, again and again.

Morning Dog Walks

I. Mystery Breed

It nests shyly in the rescue pup's breast
until one April day it wakes, grows wings
and the tentative howl of a hound
fledges from her throat.

II. Winter Dog Walk #312

It's one of those analytical walks
where she scrutinizes every scent
and sorts the ingredients
        like a wine-taster, or a chemist.

She's a student of modern history
conducting research with her nose,
learning precisely
        who stalked this way before.

Leashed, dragging me behind,
only her imagination can run wild.
Other dogs come alive to her through
aromatic leavings, prints punched in snow.
Ghosts of deer appear
        along wandering trails.

Furry creatures take cover as she tunnels
with her shovel-nose, or
pounces with all fours on something scurrying.
        But she's too slow, thank goodness.

We pause on the corner for the pulse and twitch
of her black muzzle. Proud in her peacock collar
her head swivels, and eyes search
        like a periscope on a submarine
as three crows in a tree scold us:

infringing on *their* territory.

Her brain is exhausted after thinking so hard.
She grows cold, grabs the pink leash in her mouth,
wrestles it down like a snake,
    and leads me home.

Why They Should Bring Back Gym Class in College

I.

Freshman year, all that's left
is Diving.

Every week, twice a week, I wait in a snake line of women
and when it's my turn, and everyone's watching

scale the ladder
walk the nubby surface to the end of the plank

and do the dive, the prescribed leap of the week:
front, back, swan, jack-knife....

whether I fear slipping, tripping
or re-injuring my weak knee,

despite fears of lousy form, the embarrassment
of the belly flop, or hitting my head on the pool floor.

I face my dread over and over again
as the cold water cuts me in two

the frightened one I thought I was, left behind,
revealing the brave one I am.

II.

Next semester, all that's left
is Riflery.

I—who never held a gun—find myself
prone, kneeling, standing, rifle shouldered in arms,
braced for the kickback.

I'm a miniature militia
shooting at tiny targets on the back wall

that I collect and tape into an art collage on my dorm room wall.

Such precision: bull's eyes and near misses every time.

I'm good at something I'll never need,
something I never wanted.

Fox

Thousands of trees are down,
pounded and slammed by wind on the 4th of July.
Hundreds of others angle unnaturally like broken bones
caught swooning in the arms of others.
We count our luck in being missed.

Such destruction gives eager loggers a chance
to clear roads with chainsaws,
and forces the relocation of wildlife.

Someone saw a bear at Knudsen Dam.
Buck Brandt saw a 400 pounder
gorging on seeds at his feeder.

After a long drive, supper with watery beer
and too much grease, and a background video
of a boy and his grandfather catching a muskie,

we roll onto Cass Bluff Loop.
The scents of sweet-dusky pines, birch,
and sycamore evoke other trips down this road.

We roll our windows up to keep out
legions of insects that will surely find their way in,
specks we've been seeing in our high beams
since Bena, as we take the curves, watch for deer.

There's something in our headlights
in the middle of the road.
We slow to a crawl. It's a fox—
a kit—white chest

turned toward us. Sharp, thin bones,
rough, red fur, perked ears.
The creature stares as if expecting us.

Blinded by our lights, like an actor

unable to see the audience, it
turns and trots down the middle of the road.

We follow and notice the easy,
hopping gait. Then it veers left,
and vanishes in a puff of vegetation.
My once-tired pulse quickens.

Uncovering

Insight

It's one of those rare days where one twist of Rubik's cube
presents a whole new pattern, where the eye doctor's oculars flip
and *this one* is surprisingly clearer than *this one*, or
if you close one eye and look with the other
you create a shift in perspective, your nose moving on its own.

You slide over one key on the keyboard, and form new words.
You accidentally touch the insert button
and erase each letter as you type.
The dog walks right instead of left,
turns around, and doesn't chase the truck.

After circling in one direction and then the other,
after false starts before the gun goes off,
you come face-to-face with your greatest weakness:
the inexplicable reflex that makes you do what you later regret,
that taps the acid, the lemon, and the closeted knives
you pretend the recipients deserve.

Marquette Sunset

Pale sky over gray water,
like the rendering of the thin interior of a shell;
impermanent nuance, subtle fade of pink and blue.

I turn around and the sky opposite
is a *Gone with the Wind* sky, Atlanta burning.
Lurid magentas and golds and oranges
have been chasing me.

Sometimes it's good to turn around,
observe the background,
see the surround,
the whole of which we are a tiny part,
make space and room for being caught.

Listen to the Trees

Open your arms. Be generous.
Stand tall and brush the morning sky,
stroke the disheveled stars.
Shade and protect the small things.

Be steadfast and rooted
even when you go unnoticed.
Be grateful for your symmetry
or eccentricity.

Let your leaves unfurl like the flag of a dog's tail—
bush out, shake, and rustle,
and watch the dew find its glint on them.
Go ahead and be green, be yellow, orange or red.

When it's called for, announce yourself.
And while you're at it,
become a connoisseur of mists that follow rain—
mists like chiffon fronds curling up from the pond

to find their second sleep in you.
Let breezes have their way with you.
Stand back as fallen seeds are scooped by birds
that pause to sing or nest in you.

Let insects outnumbering men alight and light you,
live in you, pitch tents in your leafy greenness.
Let the full moon reveal itself between your bare boughs,
and bend with the wind.

And if you must break into a jagged stump—
be a miniature cathedral—with squirrels and chipmunks
chasing through your naves and apses,
with spiders spinning silver in you.

Tuesday Morning

Popples popples popples/pines pines pines/ birches birches birches

Bracken ferns/vetch/rue/Queen Anne's lace

Me riding my bike down the road/Me riding my bike down the road

Bracken ferns/vetch/rue/Queen Anne's lace—a bunny!

Popples popples popples/pines pines pines/ birches birches birches

On the Prowl

I.

You stalk wonder, pressing like snow, irrepressible,
keening with the quivering of leaves white against green,
swimming unseen with legions of fish channeling through the lake.

You want to know the feral secrets—
where deer and fawn mince beyond the highline,
where fox burrows, mouse hides,
and bear finds blue beneath the leaf.

You contemplate the cool arc and glide of a gull's wing
above the navy sea, listen to white fringe beat the shore,
yet you are so easily distracted
by the gaudy-gleam-sparkle-quickness-sound,
the blinding static of the unexplored.

II.

You find it within the wind-stirred sediment
that renders the lake bed indiscernible, within
the flaming choke-embrace of bittersweet in autumn,
in the trampled hollow where mute deer huddled,
and in parental words you were too young to question.

In things so close they're nearly invisible.

Uncoverings

Worms under soil. Bats behind shutters. Attic mice.
All the cozy, dark places where creatures settle.

*

Childhood's black gobstopper rolls in
layered with color upon color for licking.

*

Cryptic claims delight in discovery—
like green beans camouflaged within their leaves,
ready for picking.

*

We are shy. We try
for inconspicuousness,
while dreaming of public nakedness.

*

To capture and carry away—
                    charmed,
                              enthralled,
                    entranced—
ravishment first must hide.

*

Elusive rolls and scatters pills, coins, pens,
spilled beads of mercury.

*

Ah, the hidden treasure of the unexpressed,
                    the nuanced,
                              inexplicit,
                                        imprecise.

*

All around me: sureness and mystery,
          inscrutability and surprise
conspiring and colliding,

beyond floaters in my eyes.

*

Wind outs the dance of the tall grasses.
Trees hold birds in their arms
within forests of leaves.

Unheard Melody

you like to think it's mellifluous, mellow,
       legato bowed by a cello

of course it's there, and
       you'll never hear it
or if you do, you won't recognize the dialect,
otherworldly,
      foreign,
          alien

a tune made with notes you can't sing,
       composed of harmonics echoing so faintly
you have to make them up

it lives in dog-fur shine, in one internal,
       windowless room of the house you only visit,
in the thick lake of fog that never lifts

you listen for it in the rolling trills of cranes,
       in geese migrating overhead,
in blooming morning glories
       singing duets with the roses

it lights in dew, in frost, in the tops of trees,
       in cornfields shining in the sun,
just beyond the next curve, next hill

it abides in dreams,
       drops from the sky as ivory carvings,
lives in sculpture, animates art

the new baby knows the tune
       you once knew and forgot

standing at the window watching
      you cock an ear,
drift asleep listening

Land's End

The print and lines are too fine.
        I can't tell north from south.

My vision's so narrow
        I see only a few frames
and so
        make peace with a few pieces.

In the end, I exalt the partial
        the uncovering of one fragile arc,
one fractal blip, one glittering tip.

Katherine (Kathy) Edgren grew up in Grand Rapids, Michigan and was first published at the age of seventeen under her maiden name: Kathy Kool. In 2004, she was awarded first place for the *Writer's Digest* non-rhyming poetry contest, and appeared in *The Year's Best Writing* in 2005. Her poems have been published in the *Christian Science Monitor, the Birmingham Poetry Review, Barbaric Yawp, Main Channel Voices, Oracle, Bear Creek Haiku, the Coe Review,* and the *Evening Street Review.* They also appear in *Writers Reading at Sweetwaters, An Anthology, 2007, and the Poetry Society of Michigan Anthology 2016.* While Katherine is now retired, in her work life she served as a City Councilmember in Ann Arbor, Michigan, raised money for the ACLU, was a project manager on research and intervention projects in Detroit addressing asthma and air quality, and managed a department at University Health Service, the University of Michigan. Her two chapbooks were published by Finishing Line Press: "Transports," and "Long Division." In addition to writing, she loves to bike, garden, hike, swim, sing, and walk her dog. She lives in Dexter with her husband, and has two grown children and two grandchildren.

CPSIA information can be obtained
at www.ICGtesting.com
Printed in the USA
FFOW03n0627251017
41472FF